300 QUESTIONS
LDS Couples Should Ask

for a more

Vibrant Marriage

300 QUESTIONS
LDS Couples Should Ask
for a more
Vibrant Marriage

SHANNON ALDER

Horizon Publishers
Springville, Utah

ISBN 13: 978-0-88290-976-9

Published by Horizon Publishers, an imprint of Cedar Fort, Inc., 2373 W. 700 S., Springville, UT 84663
Distributed by Cedar Fort, Inc. www.cedarfort.com

LIBRARY OF CONGRESS CATALOGING-IN-PUBLICATION DATA

Alder, Shannon L.
  300 questions for a more vibrant marriage / Shannon L. Alder.
    p. cm.
  ISBN 978-0-88290-976-9
  1. Marriage--Religious aspects--Church of Jesus Christ of Latter-day
Saints. I. Title.

  BX8641.A43 2011
  248.8'440882893--dc22

                        2010042240

Cover design by Danie Romrell
Cover design © 2011 by Lyle Mortimer
Edited and typeset by Melissa J. Caldwell

Printed in the United States of America

10 9 8 7 6 5 4 3 2 1

Printed on acid-free paper

I dedicate this book to my beautiful boys,
Arizona and Indiana.

Be selective with whom you marry
and then do everything to bring them joy
every day you are together.

CONTENTS

Let us not live a life . . . that would bring regret. . . . It is not going to matter very much how much money you made, what kind of a house you lived in, what kind of a car you drove, the size of your bank account—any of those things. What is going to matter is that dear woman who has walked with you side by side as your companion through all of the years of life and those children and grandchildren and great-grandchildren and their faithfulness and their looking to you . . . with respect and love and deference and kindness.

GORDON B. HINCKLEY

("Inspirational Thoughts," *Ensign*, Mar. 2006, 3–4)

Marriage is meant to be and must be a loving, binding, harmonious relationship between a man and a woman. When a husband and a wife understand that the family is ordained of God and that marriage can be filled with promises and blessings extending into the eternities, separation and divorce would seldom be a consideration in the Latter-day Saint home. Couples would realize that the sacred ordinances and covenants made in the house of the Lord provide the means whereby they can return to the presence of God.

W. DOUGLAS SHUMWAY

("Marriage and Family: Our Sacred Responsibility,"
Ensign, May 2004, 95)

INTRODUCTION

I have a friend whose marriage I admire. While I'm sure that she and her husband have their share of differences, they seem to enjoy being with each other. They've been married for thirty-two years, and despite the wrinkling skin, graying hair, and widening waists, their affection appears to have deepened. In fact, they even seem to embrace the aging process. They have always seemed so "in sync."

Which is why I was surprised by what she recently told me. Throughout their marriage her husband had always worked, until just recently when he decided to go back to school to become a college professor. Although she knew her husband was getting restless in his current career, she wasn't quite prepared for his announcement that he wanted to quit his job to pursue a dream he had as a teenager.

He tried to make it clear that this was something she should have seen coming. But this was news to her. He was at that famous "midlife" stage and wanted to try something different before it was too late.

She did her best to be understanding. In fact, she did understand. But she still felt overwhelmed with having to find a part-time job to put him through school. She felt betrayed. To her, this seemed to come out of left field. She felt like she was living with a stranger.

Through prayer, communication, and patience, they are making things work. They are slowly, together, working their way toward a new understanding. It was an important lesson for me. Everyone talks about people changing and growing over time. And the same is true of a marriage. New situations arise, and circumstances change. Communication is key for a marriage to survive. Yet some husbands and wives are surprised to find that there are still things to learn about each other, even after several years of marriage.

The truth is, we are all evolving and changing as people through circumstances, outside influences, and the very art of aging. It's important to "keep up" with each other and to be aware of where the other is in their head. That takes time, desire, and skill. As Latter-day Saints, we live in a world where the adversary wants our marriages to fail.

Did you know?

- 82 percent of all married couples will reach their fifth wedding anniversary, but only 52 percent will celebrate fifteen years of marriage.

- Children who are raised in single-parent homes are less likely to marry and more likely to divorce.

- Teen girls from single-parent homes are twice as likely to drop out of high school or give birth to a child out of wedlock.

- Teenage marriages are even more prone to divorce than the national average of 50 percent. Their divorce rate is 65 percent.

- About 60 percent of men and 40 percent of women will have an affair at some point in their marriage.

These statistics can be scary, but they don't need to be proven in your marriage. I was married at age nineteen, and I have been together with my best friend for twenty-one years. I had all sorts of odds against my teen marriage failing. Our marriage has survived me growing up from a teenager to an adult. We have had our share of fights and make ups, ups and downs, and everything in between. However, we remain committed to staying together because of our faith and friendship, but most important, because of our constant open dialog. There is nothing we can't talk about.

A great way to stay on track is to have simple conversations and dialogs that will bring back the sparks you both felt during the dating stage.

Elder Hugh B. Brown has written: "Where there is deep and mature love, which is being nurtured and jealously guarded, the couple will confide in each other and discuss all matters of joint interest—and in marriage everything should be of interest to both— they will stand together in adversity, will lean on, support, and give strength to each other. They will find that their combined strength is more than double the strength of either one of them alone."[1]

Whether you have known each other for years or are newlyweds, use these questions as a road map to reconnect with your spouse. You will experience openness, laughter, closeness, and deeper understanding of each another, which will lead you on the path to a vibrant marriage. You don't have to get every question right to feel like your marriage is a success. You just have to listen to what your spouse feels and learn about one another. Marriage is a process, not a destination. Through faith, honesty, communication, and love, you can solve most any problem!

NOTE

1. Hugh B. Brown, *You and Your Marriage* (Salt Lake City: Bookcraft, 1960), 30.

As we go through life, even through very rough waters, a father's instinctive impulse to cling tightly to his wife or to his children may not be the best way to accomplish his objective. Instead, if he will lovingly cling to the Savior and the iron rod of the gospel, his family will want to cling to him and to the Savior. . . . This lesson is surely not limited to fathers. Regardless of gender, marital status, or age, individuals can choose to link themselves directly to the Savior, hold fast to the rod of His truth, and lead by the light of that truth. By so doing, they become examples of righteousness to whom others will want to cling.

RUSSEL M. NELSON
("Set in Order Thy House," *Ensign*, Nov. 2001, 69)

Rekindling the *Romance* and *Intimacy* in Your Marriage

What does it mean to love someone with all your heart? It means to love with all your emotional feelings and with all your devotion. Surely when you love your wife with all your heart, you cannot demean her, criticize her, find fault with her, or abuse her by words, sullen behavior, or actions. . . . What does it mean to "cleave unto her"? It means to stay close to her, to be loyal and faithful to her, to communicate with her, and to express your love for her. Love means being sensitive to her feelings and needs. She wants to be noticed and treasured. She wants to be told that you view her as lovely and attractive and important to you. Love means putting her welfare and self-esteem as a high priority in your life.

EZRA TAFT BENSON

("To the Fathers in Israel," *Ensign*, Nov. 1987, 50)

1. What things are essential for creating a romantic evening? What number one thing would ruin a romantic evening?

_____

_____

_____

_____

_____

_____

_____

2. When was the last time you went on a date?

_____

3. Do you feel that you go out on dates enough? Do you go out once a week or once a month? Does the frequency differ from your spouse's opinion? Do other couples go out more often then you do?

_____

_____

_____

_____

4. If your date night has fallen into a rut, what are three unique dates you would like to go on?

_____

_____

_____

_____

5. If you could plan the most romantic date, what would it involve?

_____

_____

_____

_____

_____

_____

_____

6. When was the last time you were on a double date? Who could you invite to go on a double date? What would you do?

_____

_____

_____

_____

_____

_____

7. What is the worst date you've gone on together?

_____

_____

_____

_____

_____

_____

8. What are some date night ideas that don't cost any money?

_____

_____

_____

_____

_____

_____

_____

_____

9. Who is more romantic in your relationship? What three things could your spouse do to be more romantic this week?

_____

_____

_____

_____

_____

_____

10. Do you believe in public displays of affection? _____

11. How affectionate are you with your spouse? Do other people perceive you to be in love with each other or distant from each another?

_____

_____

_____

_____

12. Do you hold hands when you're at church or in public? Why or why not?

_____

_____

_____

_____

_____

13. In what ways does your spouse express affection differently to you? Do you feel you love more deeply than he or she does?

_____

_____

_____

_____

_____

14. Where and when do you and your spouse have intimate talks? Does your spouse pick inappropriate times?

_____

_____

_____

_____

_____

15. Does your spouse celebrate Valentine's Day or anniversaries with as much devotion as you, or do you wish he or she would do more for you on these special days?

_____

_____

_____

16. What is the best gift your spouse has given you? Why did you like it?

_____

_____

_____

_____

_____

_____

17. What was the last compliment you gave to your spouse?

_____

_____

_____

_____

_____

18. What romantic words do you wish your spouse would say more often to you?

_____

_____

_____

_____

_____

_____

_____

19. Can you talk to your spouse openly about sex? When was the last time you talked about it?

_____

_____

_____

_____

_____

_____

20. How often would you like to have sex? Why?

_____

_____

_____

_____

_____

_____

_____

21. What are three things your spouse does during sex that turn you off? What three things turn you on?

_____

_____

_____

_____

_____

_____

_____

22. Is romance important in a couple's everyday life? If so, what is the best way to keep it alive?

_____

_____

_____

_____

_____

23. Are you currently comfortable with your body? If not, what would you change to make you comfortable? How can your spouse support you?

_____

_____

_____

_____

_____

_____

24. Does your spouse initiate lovemaking more often than you do? If so, why?

_____

_____

_____

_____

_____

_____

_____

_____

25. Do you wish your spouse would touch you more? What signals is your spouse missing from you?

_____

_____

_____

_____

_____

_____

_____

26. When do you like to be touched by your spouse? When don't you?

_____

_____

_____

_____

27. Do you want to try something new sexually with your spouse? What is something you do during lovemaking that you would prefer more of?

_____

_____

_____

_____

_____

_____

_____

28. Is it more important that your spouse thinks you're a good lover or that you think they are? Why?

_____

_____

_____

_____

_____

_____

_____

_____

29. How much absence in your relationship do you think makes your heart grow fonder?

_____

_____

_____

_____

_____

30. What is the most romantic thing you have ever done? What has your spouse done?

_____

_____

_____

_____

_____

_____

_____

_____

31. How many times during your marriage have you felt more in love than when you first met?

_____

_____

32. What do you do to take care of your appearance so your spouse will be sexually attracted to you?

_____

_____

_____

_____

_____

33. Are sexual aids such as Viagra a turn-off to you, or do you feel they would help your intimacy? Why?

_____

_____

_____

_____

34. Do you withhold sex as an instrument of manipulation or punishment in your relationship to get what you want? _____

35. When was the last time you were unpredictable when it came to sex? How does your spouse feel about that?

_____

_____

_____

36. Do you think there's a difference between love, romance, and sex? How do you define each of those terms?

_____

_____

_____

_____

_____

_____

_____

_____

37. What is the difference between sexuality and sensuality?

_____

_____

_____

_____

_____

_____

_____

38. What is the difference between having sex and making love?

_____

_____

_____

_____

_____

_____

39. What words do you want to hear during lovemaking?

_____

_____

_____

_____

_____

_____

40. What are the two most sensitive parts of your body?

_____

_____

_____

41. What are some loving ways you can tell your partner that you're not in the mood?

_____

_____

_____

_____

_____

_____

_____

_____

_____

_____

_____

42. Has the role of sex changed over the years in your marriage? What's changed? Are these changes for the better or for the worse?

_____

_____

_____

_____

_____

_____

_____

_____

_____

43. Have you ever had an unpleasant sexual experience with your spouse that you wished you could have talked about? _____

44. If you were ill or had an injury that prevented you from having sex ever again, would your spouse leave you because of it? Would he or she adjust to it?

_____

_____

_____

_____

45. Are you visual with regard to sex? Would you lose interest in your spouse if you had failing eyesight?

_____

_____

_____

46. Has there been an occasion where you wanted sex and your spouse didn't? Would you rather have your spouse turn you down or go through the motions for your benefit?

_____

_____

_____

_____

_____

_____

47. If you were bored with your partner during sex, in what ways could you change your feelings? What could your spouse do differently?

_____

_____

_____

_____

_____

48. What is the longest length of time you have had sex? Do you wish lovemaking lasted longer?

_____

_____

_____

49. Which one of you is responsible for contraceptives? Why?

_____

_____

_____

_____

50. If you could vary the place or time you have sex, which would you change? Why?

_____

_____

_____

_____

_____

51. If your spouse was having sexual problems, would you seek medical help to fix the situation? _____

52. What part of your body is the most attractive to your spouse? Why?

_____

_____

_____

53. Are there different positions you would like to try? What are they?

_____

_____

_____

_____

_____

54. How would you like your children to find out about sex? Who would talk to them about it?

_____

_____

_____

_____

Reexamining Your *Views* and *Beliefs* in Your Marriage

Essential to your success and happiness is the advice "Choose your friends with caution." We tend to become like those whom we admire, and they are usually our friends. We should associate with those who, like us, are planning not for temporary convenience, shallow goals, or narrow ambition—but rather with those who value the things that matter most, even eternal objectives.

THOMAS S. MONSON
("Be Thou an Example," *Ensign*, May 2005, 113)

1. What is your current view of how your marriage is going? Is it rocky, wonderful, or in need of improvement? Would your spouse say the same thing?

_____

_____

_____

_____

_____

2. What does quality time alone and together mean to you? Does your relationship have equal amounts of quality time spent together as a couple and alone? What would you change?

_____

_____

_____

_____

_____

_____

_____

3. Which things in life give you the most joy in your relationship?

_____

_____

_____

_____

_____

_____

4. What things in life make you most angry? What three things can you do to change these for the better?

_____

_____

_____

_____

_____

_____

_____

5. Over the years love is supposed to grow. What things have happened in your marriage that caused your spouse to love you more?

_____

_____

_____

_____

_____

_____

6. What are some of your happiest memories of your married life together so far?

_____

_____

_____

_____

_____

_____

7. Do you feel your spouse is fulfilling his or her role in the home? If not, what areas do you think he or she could improve on? What about yourself?

_____

_____

_____

_____

_____

8. If both of you have jobs outside of the home, is it working for your family? Is there anything you would change?

_____

_____

_____

_____

_____

_____

9. Does your spouse spend too much time away from the family? What things would you change so you can spend more time with your spouse and children?

_____

_____

_____

_____

_____

_____

10. Is it okay in your marriage for your spouse to have friends of the opposite sex? If not, why does that frighten you?

_____

_____

_____

_____

_____

11. Do you and your spouse see eye to eye on raising your children? What three areas could you improve on?

_____

_____

_____

_____

_____

_____

12. Do you make your partner responsible for your feelings? How do you take ownership of how you feel in every situation?

_____

_____

_____

_____

_____

13. Are you or your spouse the type to hold onto the past and bring it up in future arguments? What boundaries could you put on fights to prevent that from happening?

_____

_____

_____

_____

_____

_____

14. In what areas of your life do you need support but feel your spouse is not giving you enough? What three things could your spouse support you on now?

_____

_____

_____

_____

_____

_____

15. What aspects of yourself do you not like? How could your spouse change how you feel?

_____

_____

_____

_____

_____

16. What pastimes or hobbies did you do before you got married that you wish you did now?

_____

_____

_____

_____

_____

_____

17. What will you do if one of you really likes to hang out with a certain person or couple and the other doesn't? Is there a compromise?

_____

_____

_____

_____

_____

18. What couples in your neighborhood do you wish you were friends with? Why?

_____

_____

_____

_____

_____

_____

19. If you limit some communication from your partner, is your primary intention to protect yourself from your fears? Do you use some form of controlling behavior such as blame, withdrawal of love, threats, criticism, anger, compliance, or resistance? If so, why?

_____

_____

_____

_____

_____

20. Is having power over your partner and winning arguments more important to you than being loving to yourself and your partner? Why or why not? What was the last fight that you had where you did this?

_____

_____

_____

_____

_____

21. Are you over-obsessed with things in your life that take time away from the family? What three steps can you take to overcome this obsession this week? This month?

_____

_____

_____

_____

_____

_____

22. Are you more devoted to mutuality, caring, and sharing love than to winning, having your way, being right, or making your partner responsible for your feelings? _____

23. What random acts of kindness have you carried out this week for your spouse?

_____

_____

_____

_____

_____

_____

_____

24. Do your parents or parents-in-law interfere with your marriage? If so, what things can you do to prevent that from happening?

_____

_____

_____

_____

_____

25. When you are sick and feeling poorly, how do you like to be taken care of? Do you like to be alone, or do you like to be pampered and have someone close to your side most of the time? Why?

_____

_____

_____

_____

26. Which do you think should govern decisions, logic or emotion? Why?

_____

_____

_____

_____

_____

_____

27. Do you have sit-down meals with your spouse and family? Why or why not? What can you do to incorporate more meals together with your family this week?

_____

_____

_____

_____

_____

_____

28. On what topics do you feel qualified at giving advice? Do you listen to the advice that your spouse gives you? Why or why not?

_____

_____

_____

_____

_____

_____

29. Would it make any difference with your kids if only one of you worked? Why?

_____

_____

_____

_____

_____

30. What is your number one priority? Is it your spouse, your children, or job? Why?

_____

_____

_____

_____

_____

_____

_____

31. When was the last time you told your spouse you loved him or her and meant it?

_____

_____

32. When was the last time you actually said the words "I love you" to your children? Do you do this daily?

_____

_____

_____

33. How does your spouse discipline the children? Do you approve?

_____

_____

_____

_____

_____

_____

_____

34. Analyze the way you talk to your spouse. Is your communication respectful, or does it show disrespect? Do the children notice how you interact? How does this affect them?

_____

_____

_____

_____

_____

_____

_____

35. If you're a working mother, do you resent working, or do you enjoy your career? How does this affect your family?

_____

_____

_____

_____

_____

36. Who are the friends that you wish you still had? Did you give them up for your marriage? What can you do to better maintain friendships?

_____

_____

_____

_____

_____

_____

37. Choose a couple you think have a perfect marriage. Who are they? How far are you from having a marriage like theirs? Why?

_____

_____

_____

_____

_____

_____

38. If you could change only one thing in your life, what would that be and why?

_____

_____

_____

_____

_____

39. In a regular day, what do you find yourself thinking the most about? Is it your marriage, family, job, or hobbies? Why?

_____

_____

_____

_____

_____

40. What things in your life bring you the greatest pleasure? Greatest displeasure? Is there a balance between the two? If not, what three things would you change?

_____

_____

_____

_____

_____

_____

_____

41. What do you feel is the greatest accomplishment in your life? Did other people help make that happen?

_____

_____

_____

_____

_____

42. In what settings are you the most eager, happiest, most comfortable, saddest, and most afraid?

_____

_____

_____

_____

_____

_____

_____

_____

43. Have the things you look forward to doing each day changed over the past few years? Why or why not?

_____

_____

_____

_____

44. What are two things that you appreciate about your marriage, and why do these things seem significant?

_____

_____

_____

_____

_____

_____

45. Do you believe in karma? Soul mates? Destiny? Is marriage a process of evolution? What do you think?

_____

_____

_____

_____

_____

_____

46. What is the best relationship advice that you have ever been given? Do you seek advice outside your marriage for answers or keep your personal life private?

_____

_____

_____

_____

_____

47. Do you and your spouse agree about finances? If not, what three things can you do differently this month?

_____

_____

_____

_____

_____

_____

48. Under what circumstances would you move for your spouse? Would moving lessen your love for your spouse by going? Would you resent him or her?

---

49. Would you give up your job for your spouse? Why or why not? By doing so, how would this affect your feelings for your spouse?

---

50. If you found out one of your children had tried drugs, how would you discipline them? How would your spouse discipline them?

---

51. If you found out one of your children had premarital sex, how would you discipline him or her? How would your spouse discipline him or her?

_____

_____

_____

_____

_____

_____

_____

52. Are chores divided evenly among your family members? Does one person do more than the others?

_____

_____

_____

_____

53. If one of your teenagers became pregnant, how would you handle the situation? Would this situation tear apart your marriage? Have you spoken to your children about premarital sex?

_____

_____

_____

_____

_____

_____

Men and women joined together in marriage need to work together as a full partnership. However, a full and equal partnership between men and women does not imply the roles played by the two sexes are the same in God's grand design for His children. As the proclamation clearly states, men and women, though spiritually equal, are entrusted with different but equally significant roles. These roles complement each other. Men are given stewardship over the sacred ordinances of the priesthood. To women, God gives stewardship over bestowing and nurturing mortal life, including providing physical bodies for God's spirit children and guiding those children toward a knowledge of gospel truths. These stewardships, equally sacred and important, do not involve any false ideas about domination or subordination. Each stewardship is essential for the spiritual progression of all family members, parents and children alike.

M. RUSSELL BALLARD

("The Sacred Responsibilities of Parenthood," *Ensign*, Mar. 2006, 29–30)

Strengthening Your
Spiritual Path

In true marriage there must be a union of minds as well as of hearts. Emotions must not wholly determine decisions, but the mind and the heart, strengthened by fasting and prayer and serious consideration, will give one a maximum chance of marital happiness.

SPENCER W. KIMBALL
("The Importance of Celestial Marriage," *Ensign*, Oct. 1979, 3)

Husbands and wives who love each other will find that love and loyalty are reciprocated. This love will provide a nurturing atmosphere for the emotional growth of children. Family life should be a time of happiness and joy that children can look back on with fond memories and associations.

EZRA TAFT BENSON
("Salvation—A Family Affair," *Ensign*, Jul. 1992, 2)

1. What was the most spiritual experience you have had? What about your spouse?

_____

_____

_____

_____

_____

_____

2. How has your spirituality changed since you got married?

_____

_____

_____

_____

_____

_____

3. Do your children have a testimony of the gospel? What five things have you done as parents to show your children that you have a testimony of your faith?

_____

_____

_____

_____

_____

_____

4. What is your testimony of the Church? Does it differ from your spouse's?

_____

_____

_____

_____

_____

5. What person has influenced your spiritual life the most?

_____

6. If you could sit down with God and ask one question, what would it be?

_____

_____

_____

7. How do you show spirituality in the home?

_____

_____

_____

_____

8. How has your spouse inspired you to be a better person and seek a relationship with God?

_____

_____

_____

9. When was the last time you went to the temple as a couple? Would you like to go more?

_____

_____

10. What is the best conversation you've had about the Church?

_____

_____

_____

_____

_____

11. What calling did your spouse have that he or she excelled at?

_____

_____

12. What was your spouse's best experience from his or her mission?

_____

_____

_____

_____

_____

_____

_____

_____

13. How are you preparing for the celestial kingdom?

_____

_____

_____

_____

_____

_____

_____

14. What beliefs would your spouse go out on a limb for? Are they the same as yours?

_____

_____

_____

_____

_____

15. What things do you pray for in your marriage?

_____

_____

_____

_____

_____

_____

16. What do you feel is the most spiritual thing your spouse has done?

_____

_____

_____

_____

_____

_____

_____

_____

17. How do your prayers affect your spouse's testimony? What do they say about yourself?

_____

_____

_____

_____

_____

18. What things in life make you doubt your testimony?

_____

_____

_____

_____

_____

_____

_____

_____

19. When was the last talk you had with your children about Heavenly Father's plan?

_____

_____

20. If one of your children decided not to go on a church mission, how would you feel about it? Why?

_____

_____

_____

_____

_____

_____

21. What has been your favorite calling in the Church? Why?

_____

_____

_____

_____

_____

_____

22. Do your children bear their testimony at church? Why or why not?

_____

_____

23. Do you bear your testimony often to others? Why or why not?

_____

_____

_____

24. If you could choose any calling at church, what would it be? Why?

_____

_____

_____

_____

_____

_____

25. What money have you put away for a couple's mission?

_____

_____

_____

26. Do you want to go on a couple's mission when you retire?

_____

27. If you could go anywhere on a couple's mission, where would that be? Why?

_____

_____

_____

_____

28. If one of your children told you he or she had homosexual desires, how would you counsel him or her?

_____

_____

_____

_____

_____

_____

_____

29. How do your children view your marriage (happy, sad, turbulent, silent, unloving)? Why?

_____

_____

_____

_____

_____

_____

30. How would you feel if your child dated someone that was not of your faith?

_____

_____

_____

_____

31. Do you dress modestly? How does what you wear affect your children's choices?

_____

_____

_____

32. Do you feel you do enough to help out in your ward? Why or why not?

_____

_____

_____

_____

_____

33. If your marriage was a sermon, what would the message of your life together be?

_____

_____

_____

_____

34. Why do you attend church?

_____

_____

_____

_____

_____

35. What is your spouse's favorite scripture? Why?

_____

_____

_____

_____

_____

36. How do you support your spouse in his or her callings?

_____

_____

_____

37. When was the last time you received a special blessing of comfort? _____

38. Does your spouse live the Word of Wisdom? Are there things that have changed since you got married?

_____

_____

_____

_____

_____

39. How do you determine what is the right thing to do in life? Is God or the world your measure?

_____

_____

_____

_____

_____

40. What is your most memorable experience speaking in church? What is your spouse's?

_____

_____

_____

_____

_____

41. If something or somebody doesn't fit your spouse's spiritual beliefs, what does he or she do?

_____

_____

_____

_____

_____

_____

42. Has the Holy Ghost ever given you a warning about something to avoid or to do? Did you ignore the promptings or act on them?

_____

_____

_____

_____

_____

43. What crisis has pushed you and your spouse closer in your marriage?

_____

_____

44. Which of the Ten Commandments is the most important to you? What is your spouse's or children's?

_____

_____

_____

_____

45. Have you or your spouse changed any deeply held beliefs because of an experience you have had? What was it?

_____

_____

_____

46. What teachings of the Church confuse you? How does your spouse help you with this?

_____

_____

_____

_____

_____

_____

_____

47. Who is the most spiritual person you have met in your ward? What makes them special to you?

_____

_____

_____

_____

48. How did you come to join the Church? If you were born into it, when did you know that it was true?

_____

_____

_____

_____

_____

_____

49. What is the funniest thing that has happened in your ward?

_____

_____

_____

_____

50. Which spiritual leader in the Church do you wish you could learn more about? _____

51. What do you wish your parents had taught you about spirituality that they failed to do?

_____

_____

_____

_____

_____

_____

52. What have you and your spouse given up for your religion?

_____

_____

_____

_____

_____

_____

53. What would you change about your home ward? How can you bring about that change?

_____

_____

_____

_____

_____

_____

_____

_____

54. Which person from the Book of Mormon do you most admire? From the Bible? Why?

_____

_____

_____

_____

_____

_____

55. When in your life have you felt forgiven for something you have done?

_____

_____

_____

_____

_____

56. Have you ever tried to convert someone to the Mormon faith?

_____

57. Has anyone ever made fun of you for your beliefs? How has that changed you?

_____

_____

_____

_____

_____

_____

_____

58. Why do you think bad things happen to good people?

_____

_____

_____

_____

_____

_____

59. Do you think the world is becoming more spiritual or less spiritual? Why?

_____

_____

_____

_____

_____

_____

60. What key principle do you think is the most important for people to learn in this world: respect, love, community, honoring parents, or something else? Why?

_____

_____

_____

_____

_____

_____

61. What five things do you want to change in your spiritual life right now?

_____

_____

_____

_____

_____

62. What five things do you want to change to help your family grow together spiritually?

_____

_____

_____

_____

_____

_____

_____

63. How have you prepared your children for the wickedness in the world?

_____

_____

_____

_____

_____

64. How often do you read your scriptures? If not often, why is that?

_____

_____

_____

_____

_____

_____

_____

65. How often do you have family prayers with your spouse and family? How can you make it a daily practice?

_____

_____

_____

_____

_____

_____

*You men who hold the priesthood of God, honor your wives.
Respect them. They are the mothers of your children. When
all is said and done, when you have lived your lives and go on
to eternity, you will not take five cents of wealth that you have
accumulated, not five cents. There is only one thing that you can
take with you, and that is your eternal soul and the love and
companionship of your husband or your wife. Live worthy of it.*

GORDON B. HINCKLEY
("Inspirational Thoughts," *Ensign,* Mar. 2006, 4)

*Be wise with your families. Be wise in fulfilling your Church
callings. Be wise with your time. Be wise in balancing all of your
responsibilities. O be wise, my beloved brothers and sisters. What
can I say more?*

—M. RUSSELL BALLARD
("O Be Wise," *Ensign,* Nov. 2006, 20)

Reacquainting *Yourself* with your *Spouse*

The most important single thing that any Latter-day Saint ever does in this world is to marry the right person, in the right place, by the right authority.

—Bruce R. McConkie
("Agency or Inspiration?" *New Era*, Jan. 1975, 38.)

One good yardstick as to whether a person might be the right one for you is this: in her presence, do you think your noblest thoughts, do you aspire to your finest deeds, do you wish you were better than you are?

Ezra Taft Benson
("To the Single Adult Brethren of the Church," *Ensign*, May 1988, 53)

1. Which of the following things do you know about your spouse from the list below?

Birthday:

Birth City:

Dream Place to Visit:

Favorite Food:

Favorite Drink:

Favorite Restaurant:

Favorite Stores:

Favorite Color:

Favorite Sport or Team:

Favorite Vacation Spot:

Favorite Movie:

Favorite Bible Story:

Favorite Book of Mormon Story:

Favorite Season of the Year:

Favorite TV Show:

Favorite City:

Favorite Song/Singer/Band:

Favorite Cartoon Character:

Favorite Bible Character:

Favorite Authors:

Favorite Artists:

Favorite Flowers:

2. What is the funniest thing your spouse has done?

_____

_____

_____

_____

3. What five things has your spouse done in his or her life that you are most proud of?

_____

_____

_____

_____

_____

_____

_____

4. Is there anyone or anything your spouse would be willing to die for?

_____

_____

5. What kind of talents does your spouse have? Do your children have these same talents? What are their talents?

_____

_____

_____

_____

6. What kind of hobbies does your spouse have? Do you have similar interests?

_____

_____

_____

_____

_____

_____

_____

7. Who are your spouse's three closest friends? How did they meet?

_____

_____

_____

_____

_____

8. What makes your spouse sad? What makes your spouse happy?

_____

_____

_____

_____

_____

_____

9. What qualities do you admire in your spouse as a mate? Have these qualities changed over time?

_____

_____

_____

_____

_____

_____

_____

10. What is one thing your spouse admires about each of his or her parents?

_____

_____

_____

_____

11. What are the good and bad qualities that your spouse has passed on to your children?

_____

_____

_____

_____

_____

_____

_____

12. Which family members does your spouse buy birthday or special holiday gifts for (such as parents, siblings, aunts/uncles, grandparents, cousins, and so on)? Do you feel he or she gives too much?

_____

_____

_____

_____

_____

_____

13. What would your spouse say has been the best period during your marriage? If that time is not now, why is that?

_____

_____

_____

_____

_____

14. What secrets do you know about your spouse that no one else knows?

_____

_____

_____

_____

_____

_____

_____

_____

15. When does your spouse have the hardest time saying he or she is sorry?

_____

_____

_____

_____

_____

16. What are your spouse's favorite smells and sounds? What memories or emotions do they evoke?

_____

_____

_____

_____

_____

_____

17. What book, movie, song, or work of art changed the way your spouse looks at the world? Why?

_____

_____

_____

_____

_____

_____

18. Who in your spouse's life influenced him or her the most during his or her childhood? How?

_____

_____

_____

_____

_____

_____

19. Who talks more, you or your spouse? _____

20. Are you and your spouse night owls or early birds? Why is that?

_____

_____

_____

_____

_____

_____

21. What is the favorite meal your spouse likes to make for you? What is the favorite meal you have made for your spouse?

_____

_____

_____

22. When was the last time your spouse wrote you a love letter?

_____

_____

23. Which character in a book or a movie is a lot like your spouse?

_____

_____

_____

_____

24. If your spouse wanted to learn a foreign language and travel to a different country, what would it be and where would he or she go?

_____

_____

_____

_____

25. What part of your home does your spouse claim as his or her private space?

_____

_____

_____

_____

26. What games or sports is your spouse best at playing?

_____

_____

_____

_____

27. What qualities do you admire in your spouse as a parent?

_____

_____

_____

_____

28. Would your spouse rather be handsome/beautiful or incredibly wise? Why?

_____

_____

_____

29. What is the nicest thing your spouse has ever done for you?

_____

_____

_____

_____

_____

30. What chore does your spouse dread doing the most? Do you ever switch chores to give your spouse a break?

_____

_____

_____

_____

_____

_____

31. What was the best thing that happened in your spouse's childhood?

_____

_____

_____

_____

_____

_____

32. Who is the best teacher your spouse ever had in school?

_____

33. Which one of the world's cultures does your spouse find to be the most interesting and fascinating? Why?

_____

_____

_____

_____

_____

34. Which prophet, Church general authority, or influential speaker does your spouse admire the most? Is it the same as you?

_____

_____

_____

35. Which historical figure, alive or dead, would your spouse liked to have met? What would he or she ask this person?

_____

_____

36. What would your spouse say was your love song when you first met? _____

37. What are your spouse's worst childhood memories?

_____

_____

_____

_____

_____

38. What are your spouse's favorite family traditions? Have you incorporated these into your marriage?

_____

_____

_____

_____

_____

_____

_____

39. What are your spouse's political beliefs?

_____

_____

_____

_____

_____

_____

40. What kind of relationship does your spouse have with his or her parents? With his or her siblings?

_____

_____

_____

_____

_____

41. If your spouse could relive one day of your marriage, what day would it be?

_____

_____

_____

_____

_____

_____

_____

42. If your spouse could relive one day of his or her youth, what day would it be?

_____

_____

_____

_____

_____

_____

43. What three adjectives best describe your spouse? Why?

_____

_____

_____

_____

_____

_____

44. What do you remember about your spouse when you first met?

_____

_____

_____

_____

_____

_____

45. What is the most attractive quality your spouse has in his or her personality? Why?

_____

_____

_____

_____

_____

_____

46. When did your spouse know that he or she wanted to marry you for all time and eternity?

_____

_____

_____

_____

_____

47. What in your marriage means the most to your spouse?

_____

_____

_____

_____

_____

48. How are you and your spouse different from each other? How are you similar?

_____

_____

_____

_____

_____

_____

_____

_____

_____

49. Is there laughter in your home? Are you funnier than your spouse? How often do you laugh together?

_____

_____

50. When your spouse gets mad, how does he or she express this? Do you wish there was another way?

_____

_____

_____

_____

_____

51. What is the best advice your spouse has given you over the years?

_____

_____

_____

_____

52. What is your favorite memory from your wedding day? What is your spouse's?

_____

_____

_____

_____

53. If your friends gave you a $50 gift card as a house-warming gift, would your spouse spend it on him or herself or buy something you both could enjoy?

_____

_____

_____

54. If your spouse could choose any career and it didn't matter how much it paid, what would he or she do?

_____

_____

_____

_____

_____

In true marriage there must be a union of minds as well as of hearts. Emotions must not wholly determine decisions, but the mind and the heart, strengthened by fasting and prayer and serious consideration, will give one a maximum chance of marital happiness.

SPENCER W. KIMBALL
(The Importance of Celestial Marriage," *Ensign*, Oct. 1979, 3)

Don't treasure up past wrongs, reprocessing them again and again. In a marriage relationship, festering is destructive; forgiving is divine (see D&C 64:9–10). Plead for the guidance of the Spirit of the Lord to forgive wrongs . . . , to overcome faults, and to strengthen relationships.

DALLIN H. OAKS
("Divorce," *Ensign*, May 2007, 72)

Reconnecting with Your Spouse during *Tough Times*

*True marriage is based on happiness . . . that comes from giving,
serving, sharing, sacrificing, and selflessness.*

SPENCER W. KIMBALL
(Relief Society Course of Study, 1987, 122)

*In order to strengthen the father in the home, I make two simple
suggestions: first, sustain and respect the father in his position;
second, give him love, understanding, and some appreciation for his
efforts. . . . In terms of giving fathers love and understanding, it
should be remembered that fathers also have times of insecurity and
doubt. Everyone knows fathers make mistakes—especially they
themselves. Fathers need all the help they can get; mostly they need
love, support, and understanding from their own.*

JAMES E. FAUST
("The Father Who Cares," *Ensign,* Sep. 2006, 4)

1. What are three topics that you don't see eye to eye on with your spouse? What could you do to see his or her point of view? Do you avoid these topics, or do you talk about them all the time?

_____

_____

_____

_____

_____

_____

_____

2. Are you and your spouse open to learning how to create a better marriage? If your spouse isn't open to this, then how are you taking care of yourself in the face of your spouse's choices? What books have you read? What counselors have you seen?

_____

_____

_____

_____

_____

_____

3. If you're the type of person who tries to change your spouse, what have you done to define your own inner worth instead of attempting to define your spouse?

_____

_____

_____

4. Do you have fears and insecurities in the marriage that you blame your partner for? What have you done to start your inner healing and to move beyond these fears?

_____

_____

_____

_____

_____

_____

_____

_____

5. Is it ever appropriate for someone to express anger in a physical way? If so, when and how? If you're in an abusive relationship, what have you done to seek help?

_____

_____

_____

_____

6. How do you fulfill your spouse so he or she won't stray?

_____

_____

_____

_____

_____

7. Have there been bad periods in your marriage that made you contemplate leaving or having an affair? When was this? How did things change for the better?

_____

_____

_____

_____

_____

_____

_____

8. What are two reasons why your spouse would marry you all over again?

_____

_____

_____

_____

9. What are three fears your spouse has about you? What are three things you can do to change those fears?

_____

_____

_____

_____

_____

_____

10. What five things in your marriage that need to change? What are three things you can do this week to change things around? What about this month?

_____

_____

_____

_____

_____

_____

_____

_____

_____

_____

11. What in your relationship makes your spouse feel guilty, sad, worried, or annoyed?

_____

_____

_____

_____

12. What three things will tear your marriage apart? What are things you can do to prevent this from happening?

_____

_____

_____

13. When does your spouse feel most respected by you? Do you respect him or her often enough? What boundaries need to be set so you don't offend your spouse?

_____

_____

_____

_____

_____

_____

14. Do you fight fair? If not, what could you change about the rules so neither of you goes overboard? What are three things you promise not to do in a fight?

_____

_____

_____

_____

_____

_____

15. If you had to let go of all areas of control in your marriage, what area would be the hardest for you? Why are you controlling in this area? How can you change your point of view?

_____

_____

_____

16. What three things have you done that have lost your spouse's trust? What are five things you can do this week to help rebuild that trust?

_____

_____

_____

_____

_____

_____

_____

_____

_____

_____

17. When the both of you fight, does your spouse feel you're determined to be right, or are you listening to him or her? Why?

_____

_____

_____

_____

18. What topics have you not discussed in your marriage and why?

_____

_____

_____

_____

19. Do you think you would prefer a calm, loving, consistent marriage or one that is full of excitement, wild times, and rocky patches? Are you in a rut? What can you do to make things exciting?

_____

_____

_____

_____

_____

_____

20. What makes your spouse feel secure and safe?

_____

_____

_____

_____

_____

_____

21. What rituals could be added to your relationship on a daily, weekly, monthly, and yearly basis that would help you and your spouse remain close?

_____

_____

_____

_____

_____

_____

22. Do you need to hear "I love you" or similar words on a regular basis from your spouse? How many times a day do you want to hear these words? How often do you want a kiss or hug from your spouse?

_____

_____

_____

_____

_____

23. If your spouse had an affair, how would you react? What would be your steps to rebuilding the situation? Could you forgive a spouse for cheating? What is your limit of forgiveness?

_____

_____

_____

_____

_____

_____

_____

24. Over the past five years, how do you think you have changed for the worse? For the better?

_____

_____

_____

_____

_____

25. What first attracted you to your spouse? How has that one attraction changed since then?

_____

_____

_____

_____

_____

_____

26. What has changed about yourself that your spouse might dislike? Would you change in order to save your marriage?

_____

_____

_____

_____

_____

_____

_____

27. Do you keep secrets from each other? What is so terrible that you can't talk to each other about?

_____

_____

_____

_____

_____

_____

28. What is your position on divorce? What circumstances would cause you to take that action? What steps would you take to prevent divorce?

_____

_____

_____

_____

_____

_____

_____

29. In what cases would you consider separation? What action would you take to prevent this?

_____

_____

_____

_____

_____

_____

_____

30. What if your spouse wanted to separate and you didn't? Would that end your marriage?

_____

_____

_____

_____

31. How do you define infidelity? Is flirting infidelity? Do you and your spouse's views differ? If so, what boundaries could you set up that would make each of you feel better?

_____

_____

_____

_____

_____

_____

_____

_____

32. What methods do you use to effect change (for example, the silent treatment, control, anger, kindness, and so on)? What is working? What is not?

_____

_____

_____

_____

33. What is your attitude toward honesty in marriage? Do you trust your spouse? What are three things you can do to make your spouse feel more secure in your relationship?

_____

_____

_____

_____

_____

34. What are five things that you can immediately do to make positive changes in your marriage this year?

_____

_____

_____

_____

_____

_____

35. What are five things your spouse does or says that prevents you from feeling the Spirit in your home? What are things he or she can do to help you feel the Spirit?

_____

_____

_____

_____

_____

_____

36. How do you and your spouse feel about abortion in the case of incest or rape?

_____

_____

_____

_____

37. If one of your teenage children got pregnant, would you support an adoption or help her raise the child?

_____

_____

_____

_____

_____

_____

38. What are your annoying habits? Do they hurt your relationship with your spouse? What are three things you can do to stop your bad habits this week?

_____

_____

_____

_____

_____

_____

39. Have you ever made abusive statements to other people about your spouse that he or she is unaware of? _____

40. If your spouse were grieving for a parent that passed away, how would you help him or her through that period of time? How does your spouse get through tough times?

_____

_____

_____

_____

_____

41. Does your spouse talk about your relationship with other people? How does that make you feel? How can you keep your relationship private? What boundaries have you set up in your relationship?

_____

_____

_____

_____

_____

_____

_____

42. Does your spouse come to you about problems or go elsewhere? What can you do to make your spouse more comfortable confiding in you?

_____

_____

_____

_____

_____

_____

43. Do you still love each other? Are you still committed to the marriage? Are you willing to make the effort to figure out how to save your marriage?

_____

_____

44. Do you still have the same feelings for your spouse that you did when you married? How have your feelings grown? How have they changed for the worse?

_____

_____

_____

_____

_____

_____

45. All a divorce will do is end your marriage and split up your family. If you want a change in the dynamics between you and your spouse, what other options can you consider?

_____

_____

_____

_____

_____

_____

_____

46. Have you thought about the negative consequences of divorce? How would you feel seeing your ex-spouse with another man or woman?

_____

_____

_____

_____

47. Do you spend time with friends who cheat on their spouses? What friendships impact your relationship in a negative way? Are you willing to distance yourself from these associations to better your marriage?

_____

_____

_____

_____

48. Do you spend time with friends who are single? How does this affect your marriage?

_____

_____

_____

_____

_____

_____

49. What are some of the factors that increase the chances of having an affair while married? What temptations are in your life now that need to change immediately?

_____

_____

_____

_____

_____

_____

50. Do you feel emotional infidelity is the same as physical infidelity? What's the difference?

_____

_____

_____

_____

_____

_____

51. What is your plan if marriage counseling fails?

_____

_____

_____

_____

_____

_____

_____

52. What were the signs over the past two years that your desire for each other was changing?

_____

_____

_____

_____

_____

_____

_____

53. Who do you need to forgive in your life?

_____

_____

_____

_____

_____

_____

54. What have you said to your spouse that you regret saying? Do you say you're sorry for the things that hurt your spouse? Or do you expect your spouse to know you're sorry without saying the words?

_____

_____

_____

_____

_____

_____

_____

_____

_____

55. When do you feel distant from your spouse?

_____

_____

_____

_____

_____

56. If you were having problems in your marriage, would you read your spouse's private journal to find out what was going wrong?

_____

57. How often do you give your spouse undivided attention? Do you pay attention to what he or she is saying?

_____

_____

_____

58. If your spouse or children have a substance abuse problem, what can you do to help them?

_____

_____

_____

_____

_____

59. What would you do if your teen or spouse had an Internet porn or chat room problem? What steps would you take to help them?

_____

_____

_____

_____

_____

_____

_____

60. What is your primary intent when asking the questions in this book? Is it to get to know your spouse better or to pick at your spouse's faults?

_____

_____

61. Do you have an anger problem? If so, to what lengths will you go to change yourself in order to save your marriage?

_____

_____

_____

_____

62. If the physical attraction that you once had for your spouse is now gone, what other qualities in him or her make up for that loss? Do you feel divorce should be granted based on loss of physical attraction, or is your relationship deeper than that? Make a list of all the things you are looking for in a person.

_____

_____

_____

_____

_____

_____

_____

_____

The family proclamation gives this beautiful explanation of the relationship between a husband and a wife: While they have separate responsibilities, "in these sacred responsibilities, fathers and mothers are obligated to help one another as equal partners."

DALLIN H. OAKS

("Priesthood Authority in the Family and the Church," *Ensign*, Nov. 2005, 26)

Marriage is sanctified when it is cherished and honored in holiness. That union is not merely between husband and wife; it embraces a partnership with God (see Matthew 19:6). "Husband and wife have a solemn responsibility to love and care for each other" ("The Family: A Proclamation to the World," paragraph 6). Children born of that marital union are "an heritage of the Lord" (Psalm 127:3). Marriage is but the beginning bud of family life; parenthood is its flower. And that bouquet becomes even more beautiful when graced with grandchildren. Families may become as eternal as the kingdom of God itself (see D&C 132:19–20).

RUSSELL M. NELSON

("Nurturing Marriage," *Ensign*, May 2006, 36)

Planning Your *Goals* and *Future* Together

In this Church the man neither walks ahead of his wife nor behind his wife but at her side. They are coequals.

EZRA TAFT BENSON
(in Conference Report, Oct. 1996, 68; or *Ensign*, Nov. 1996, 49)

Mother, who willingly made that personal journey into the valley of the shadow of death to give us birth, deserves our undying gratitude. One writer summed up our love for mother when he declared, "God could not be everywhere, and so He gave us mothers.

THOMAS S. MONSON
("An Attitude of Gratitude," *Ensign*, Feb. 2000, 4)

1. What five things do you want to change financially for your family in the next five years? In ten years?

_____

_____

_____

_____

_____

_____

_____

2. What five things do you want to change in your family life this year?

_____

_____

_____

_____

_____

_____

_____

3. What five things can you do this year that will bring your family closer to God?

_____

_____

_____

_____

4. What are three things you can do this week that will show your spouse that you love him or her?

_____

_____

_____

_____

_____

_____

_____

5. What are five things you can change in your life now that will strengthen your marriage?

_____

_____

_____

_____

_____

_____

_____

6. What are three things you can do this year that will improve your relationship with your children?

_____

_____

_____

_____

7. Where do you both want to be buried when you pass away?

_____

_____

_____

8. Do you have a living trust? _____

9. Who is the beneficiary of your will in the event of your death?

_____

_____

_____

_____

_____

_____

10. If you and your spouse were to die, who would take care of your children? _____

11. What have you not done with your spouse that you want to accomplish in the next year? In five years? In ten years?

_____

_____

_____

_____

_____

_____

_____

_____

12. If you could visit any part of the world and money wasn't an object, where would you go and how much time would you spend there? Who would you take with you?

_____

_____

_____

_____

_____

_____

13. At what age do both of you want to retire?

_____

_____

14. What do both of you envision retirement to be like?

_____

_____

_____

_____

_____

_____

_____

_____

_____

_____

_____

_____

15. Do you want to live by your children when you retire, or live somewhere else? Why?

_____

_____

_____

_____

_____

16. If you could go to any historical Church site in the world, where would you visit and why?

_____

_____

_____

_____

17. If you should die before your spouse, how will he or she be taken care of? Does he or she know your financial situation and how to handle the bills? Could your spouse easily pick up where you left off?

_____

_____

_____

_____

_____

_____

_____

18. If you only had one day left on the earth, what would you do with your time?

_____

_____

_____

_____

_____

_____

_____

_____

19. What legacy do you want to leave to your children? Will it be money, time, knowledge, or family memories?

_____

_____

_____

_____

20. If you were to die tomorrow, what would you wish to tell each of your family members before you pass away?

_____

_____

_____

_____

_____

_____

_____

_____

21. If you passed away today, what would be the one thing you most regret not having said or accomplished in your life?

_____

_____

_____

_____

_____

_____

22. What hobbies could you and your spouse do together to strengthen your relationship?

_____

_____

_____

_____

23. If ten years passed, what would you be most disappointed at not having accomplished?

_____

_____

_____

_____

_____

_____

_____

_____

24. Do you plan to pay for your children's college tuition? In what circumstances would you pay for your children's cars or tuition? What can you do to help your children save money?

_____

_____

_____

_____

_____

_____

_____

25. Where are three places you want to travel to this year on vacation as a family?

_____

_____

_____

_____

_____

26. Where do you want to be in terms of your health in the next year? In five years?

_____

_____

_____

_____

_____

27. What are five goals that you want to accomplish in your career over the next year? In five years?

_____

_____

_____

_____

_____

_____

_____

_____

28. If you could be granted three wishes, what would they be?

_____

_____

_____

_____

29. What are three things you would change about your home and living situation?

_____

_____

_____

_____

_____

30. Are you happy in your career? Why or why not?

_____

_____

_____

_____

_____

31. If there was one occupation in the world that you could have, what would it be? Is it different from what you are doing now?

_____

_____

_____

_____

_____

32. Have you considered going back to school to get a different degree? How would this impact the family?

_____

_____

_____

_____

_____

33. What are the three places you would like to visit most in your country? What about abroad?

_____

_____

34. If you could live anywhere in the world, where would it be?

_____

_____

35. Do you believe in destiny? How has this influenced your relationship and the things that have happened in your life up to this point?

_____

_____

_____

_____

_____

36. If you could pick one charity in the world to devote your time to, what would it be?

_____

_____

_____

_____

37. Would you ever want to own your own company? Why or why not?

_____

_____

_____

_____

_____

38. If you could create your own company, what would it sell or offer people?

_____

_____

_____

_____

_____

_____

39. What do you fear most about getting older?

_____

_____

_____

_____

_____

_____

_____

40. What are the jobs you have had in your life that you most enjoyed?

_____

_____

_____

_____

_____

_____

41. If you had a paid sabbatical and didn't have to work for a year, what would you do with your time?

_____

_____

_____

_____

_____

_____

_____

42. If you lost your job, what would you do financially to help you stay afloat? Would your spouse go back to work to support the family?

_____

_____

_____

_____

_____

43. What are the three most important possessions that you own?

_____

_____

_____

_____

_____

_____

44. If you could pick a day in your life to live over, what day would that be?

_____

_____

_____

_____

_____

45. What are three things we can do to save money this week? Month? Year?

_____

_____

_____

_____

_____

46. Do you live within your means, or are you constantly in debt? If you're in debt, what can you do this year to change that?

_____

_____

_____

_____

_____

_____

_____

47. Some families have house rules, such as every one sits down to eat dinner together. If you were to write your house rules, what would they be?

_____
_____
_____
_____
_____
_____
_____
_____
_____
_____
_____

48. Which house rules are consistently broken? What can you do this week to change that?

_____
_____
_____
_____
_____
_____
_____
_____

49. What are everyone's assigned chores in the house? Are they fair and equal? Do you trade off? What can you do to make sure everyone is doing their part this week?

_____

_____

_____

_____

_____

_____

_____

_____

_____

_____

50. Are you having family home evening consistently? If not, what can you do to change that?

_____

_____

_____

_____

51. Are you consistently attending church? If not, why? What can you do this month so you can attend more church functions and meetings?

_____

_____

_____

_____

52. Are you prepared in case of a family emergency? Do you have a one-year supply of food? What can you do this month to prepare for an emergency?

_____

_____

_____

_____

_____

_____

*There is great power in loving, consistent, fervent family prayer.
Don't deny your families this blessing. Don't allow the strength
that comes from family prayer to slip away from you and your loved
ones through neglect.*

JOHN GROBERG
("The Power of Family Prayer," *Ensign*, May 1982, 52)

*When there is love in a marriage, there is harmony in the home;
when there is harmony in the home, there is contentment in the
community; when there is contentment in the community, there
is prosperity in the nation; when there is prosperity in the nation,
there is peace in the world.*

CHINESE PROVERB

About the Author

*S*hannon Alder is the author of the book *300 Questions LDS Couples Should Ask Before Marriage*. She majored in physical therapy at Washburn University and works as an inpatient therapist at a rehabilitation hospital in California. Her father taught her early on to question everything in life and then write it all down so others could benefit from what she learned. Because of him, writing has been her passion. However, when she is not typing away at the computer or hiking with her husband, she spends the rest of her time devoted to the two most precious things in her life—her two beautiful boys, Indiana and Arizona. They fill her life with sunshine and make every word she writes sing.

09769 6